THE ART
OF WAR

A NEW TRANSLATION

SUN TZU

CHARTWELL
BOOKS, INC.

Introduction

It is an unusual book that was written 2500 years ago in an impenetrable classical language and yet figures on the recommended reading list of the United States Marine Corps. More unusual still for it to be a favourite book of figures so contrasting as General Douglas MacArthur and Mao Zedong (Mao Tse Tung); but Sunzi's 兵法 [*Art of War*] is such a book. Moreover it has discovered a new life outside military circles in the world of modern business management. A simple internet search under '*Art of War* + business strategy' will provide hundreds of sites claiming to offer invaluable commercial insights based on this ancient text.

According to long tradition, 兵法 was written by Sun Wu, better known as Sunzi (Sun Tzu in the old style Romanization), a general and strategist in the service of King He Lü of Wu during the Spring and Autumn Annals period of ancient China (770–476 BCE). The accuracy of this version is, however, a matter of heated scholarly debate, with some experts believing that inconsistencies and anachronisms in the text point to a later date of composition, and others questioning even the existence of Sunzi as a historical figure. Further confusing the matter is the existence of a later text from the second half of the fourth century BCE, also called the *Art of War*, written by a man called Sun Bin, who was also known as Sunzi.

There is no definitive standard text of the *Art of War*; over centuries of copying, minor variations have crept in, as is the case with most ancient manuscripts. Furthermore, classical Chinese was written without punctuation, which serves to increase the number of possible readings. There are also a number of places where the text is indisputably corrupt. All this, added to the potential ambiguity of the actual language of

Contents

計篇

孫子曰：兵者，國之大事，死生之地，存亡之道，不可不察也。

故經之以五，校之以計，而索其情：一曰道，二曰天，三曰地，四曰　將，五曰法。

> **"** *There is no absolutely standard text for the* Art of War; *over centuries of copying, minor variations have crept in...* **"**

classical Chinese, means that no two interpretations of *Art of War* are alike. In this translation I have used one of the most widely accepted versions of the text from the Song Dynasty period (960–1279 CE), and where conflicting interpretations exist, have attempted to allow context and the balance of the prose to dictate my translation.

The structure of the text is generally undisputed. It is divided into 13 chapters, each addressing an aspect of organization or strategic planning. Some of these chapters are more sophisticated and clearly complete than others, indicating again the likelihood of corruption in the text. All of them, however, are at one level intensely practical, especially Sunzi's observations on interpreting the mood of soldiers (both one's own and the enemy's) from their behaviour. What is notable throughout and what raises the work far above a simple military manual is the elegance of the prose and the underlying Daoist principles. In the eyes of Sunzi, a general is no mere jobbing soldier: he is a scholar, gentleman and philosopher. The depth of meaning which this element of mysticism imparts is undoubtedly responsible for the work's continuing and universal appeal.

Sunzi Said [1]

---

[1] Throughout the text wherever Chinese names or other words appear, I have adopted the modern pinyin romanization. Thus Sunzi rather than the traditional form Sun Tzu. Although doubts may be raised about the historical authenticity of the attribution, the author of the *Art of War* is traditionally believed to be Sun Wu, known later as Sunzi, a distinguished general in the service of King He Lü of Wu in the sixth century BCE during the period known as the Spring and Autumn Annals (770–476 BCE). The content of the text and the types of warfare it describes, however, suggest to many scholars that it was in fact written in the later Warring States period (475–221 BCE).

道者, 令民于上同意者也, 可與之死, 可與之生, 民不詭也。天者, 陰陽、寒暑、時制也。地者, 高下、遠近、險易、廣狹、死生也。將者, 智、信、仁、勇、嚴也。法者, 曲制、官道、主用也。

凡此五者, 將莫不聞, 知之者勝, 不知之者不勝。故校之以計, 而索其情。曰: 主孰有道? 將孰有能? 天地孰得? 法令孰行? 兵眾孰強? 士卒孰練? 賞罰孰明? 吾以此知勝負矣。

Planning

"...War is the place where life and death meet..."

Understanding the nature of war is of vital importance to the State. War is the place where life and death meet; it is the road to destruction or survival. It demands study. War has five decisive factors, which you must take into account in your planning; you must fully understand their relevance. First is a Moral Compass; second is Heaven; third is Earth; fourth is the Commander; fifth is Regulation.

將聽吾計,用之必勝,留之;將不聽吾計,用之必敗,去之。

計利以聽,乃為之勢,以佐其外。勢者,因利而制權也。

兵者,詭道也。故能而示之不能,用而示之不用,近而示之遠,遠而 示之近。利而誘之,亂而取之,實而備之,強而避之,怒而撓之,卑而驕之,佚而勞之,親而離之,攻其不備,出其不意。此兵家之勝, 不可先傳也。

夫未戰而廟算勝者,得算多也;未戰而廟算不勝者,得算少也。多算 勝,少算不勝,而況無算乎!吾以此觀之,勝負見矣。

"The General must be possessed of wisdom, honesty, benevolence, courage and discipline."

A Moral Compass brings the people into accord with their ruler so that they will follow him in life and in death without fear.

Heaven encompasses night and day, heat and cold and the changing of the seasons.

Earth encompasses nearness and distance, ease and hindrance, wide plains and narrow gorges – matters of life or death.

The General must be possessed of wisdom, honesty, benevolence, courage and discipline.[2]

Regulation means the marshalling of the army, correct organization and control of supplies.

A General must pay attention to all five, for they represent the difference between defeat and victory.

So you must study them when laying your plans and thoroughly understand their relevance. By this I mean you should consider:
Which Ruler has a Moral Compass? Which General has ability? Which side is best favoured by climate and terrain? Where is leadership most effective? Which army is strongest? Whose officers and men are best trained? Who best understands the use of reward and punishment? The answers to these questions tell me who will succeed and who will be defeated.

---

[2] Although the *Art of War* is essentially a practical handbook, Sunzi incorporates philosophical principles from both Confucianism and Daoism. The character I have translated as "moral compass" is 道 dào which is the "True Way" of Laozi and Daoism, and clearly here shares something of the same meaning. The five qualities essential in a general are pretty much the military equivalents of the Five Confucian Virtues.

作戰篇

孫子曰：凡用兵之法，馳車千駟，革車千乘，帶甲十萬，千里饋糧，則內外之費，賓客之用，膠漆之材，車甲之奉，日費千金，然後十萬 之師舉矣。其用戰也貴勝，久則鈍兵挫銳，攻城則力屈，久暴師則國 用不足。夫鈍兵挫銳，屈力殫貨，則諸侯乘其弊而起，雖有智者，能善其後矣。故兵聞拙速，未睹巧之久也。夫兵久而國利者，未之有也。故不盡知用兵之害者，則不能盡知用兵之利也。

You should retain those of your generals who heed this advice, for they will be victorious; you should dismiss those who do not, for they will be defeated.

When planning victory according to my counsel, act according to the situation and make use of external factors. To act according to the situation is to seize the advantage by adapting one's plans.

Successful war follows the path of Deception.[3] Thus when you are able to act, feign incapacity; when deploying, feign inactivity; when you are close, appear to be far off; when you are distant, appear close. When your enemy seeks an advantage, lure him further; if he is in disorder, crush him; if he is organized, be ready for him; when he is strong, avoid him; when he is angry, goad him further; if he is humble, be over-bearing; if he is resting, harry him; if his armies are united, split them. Attack where he is unprepared, appear where you are least expected. Thus you may see that in war, surprise is the key to victory.

A victorious leader plans for many eventualities before the battle; a defeated leader plans for only a few. Many options bring victory, few options bring defeat, no options at all spell disaster.

It is by using all these considerations that I can foresee who will be victorious and who will be defeated.

---

[3] Sunzi's approach to war is entirely pragmatic; the only aim is to defeat the enemy and there is no concept of anything approaching "chivalry" in describing the means of doing so. The General's "Moral Compass" applies only to his attitude to his ruler.

善用兵者,役不再籍,糧不三載;取用于國,因糧于敵,故軍食可足 也。

國之貧于師者遠輸,遠輸則百姓貧。近師者貴賣,貴賣則百姓竭,財 竭則急於丘役。力屈、財殫,中原內虛于家。百姓之費,十去其七;

公家之費:破軍罷馬,甲冑矢弩,戟盾蔽櫓,丘牛大車,十去其六。

故智將務食于敵。食敵一鐘,當吾二十鐘;箕杆一石,當吾二十石。故殺敵者,怒也;取敵之利者,貨也。故車戰,得車十乘已上,賞其先得者,而更其旌旗,車雜而乘之,卒善而養之,是謂勝敵而益強。故兵貴勝,不貴久。

故知兵之將,民之司命,國家安危之主也。

Waging War

" *...a protracted campaign depletes the state's resources...* "

As for military operations, let us consider an army of 1000 attack chariots, 1000 heavy chariots and 100,000 armoured troops, all provisioned for a campaign of 1000 li.[4] Allowing for expenses at headquarters and the front, the entertainment of allies and guests, the cost of glue and lacquer for maintenance and the manufacture of chariots and armour, an army of 100,000 men will require a daily expenditure of 1000 jin.[5]

In waging war, victory is the prize but, if it is delayed, both troops and weapons are blunted; besieging a city exhausts your strength; a protracted campaign depletes the state's resources. With your soldiers and weapons dull, strength and resources spent, your rivals will seize their chance and rise up against you. Then, no matter how wise you are, you can turn nothing to your advantage.

Thus, although I have heard of reckless haste in war, I have never seen wise delay. Nor has any state benefitted from prolonging war. Only someone who understands the perils of waging war can also understand the best way of conducting it.

---

[4] The li is a traditional unit of length in use from the very earliest times; it has, however, varied in value at different periods. Here it equates to approx 400 metres.

[5] The character for jin 金 means "precious metal" and it is not possible to be certain whether it here refers to silver or gold, or indeed what quantity of either.

A skilled general levies troops only once and transports provisions from home only twice. He brings equipment from home but forages for food from the enemy. This is how he keeps his troops fed. Provisioning an army at a distance is a sure way of emptying the state exchequer and beggaring the populace. Prices are inflated by the presence of an army, and inflation swallows up the people's money so that tolls and taxes become oppressive. With strength sapped and wealth depleted, households are stripped bare and the people will lose 70% of their income. As for public finances: broken chariots and broken-down horses, restocking of weapons, shields and armour, draught-oxen and transport wagons, all these will account for 60% of the exchequer.

It is for these reasons that a wise general forages food from the enemy; one zhong of the enemy's food is worth 20 zhong of your own; one dan[6] of the enemy's supplies is worth 20 dan of your own. For your soldiers, anger must be the spur to killing the enemy and reward must be the stimulus to defeating them. Thus in a chariot battle, if ten chariots or more are taken, then reward the soldiers who captured the first one. Change the flags and standards on the captured chariots and add them to your own squadrons. Treat the captured soldiers well and look after them. This is the tactic of using the defeated enemy to increase your strength.

So you can now see that in war it is winning alone that matters and there is no merit in prolonging a campaign. A general who truly understands warfare controls the people's fate. He is the master of the State's security.

---

[6] The zhong was a unit of volume approximately equivalent to 40 litres, and the dan a unit of weight approximately equivalent to 50 kilograms

謀攻篇

孫子曰：凡用兵之法，全國為上，破國次之；全軍為上，破軍次之；全旅為上，破旅次之；全卒為上，破卒次之；全伍為上，破伍次之。是故百戰百勝，非善之善也；不戰而屈人之兵，善之善者也。

Strategic Offence

In considering the complete art of war, it is greatly preferable to capture a state whole rather than break it up; it is better to capture an army whole rather than break it up; it is better to capture a regiment whole rather than break it up; it is better to capture a battalion whole rather than break it up; it is better to capture a company whole rather than break it up. Using this principle, you can understand that winning a hundred victories out of a hundred battles is not the ultimate achievement; the ultimate achievement is to defeat the enemy without even coming to battle.

"...the ultimate achievement is to defeat the enemy without even coming to battle..."

故上兵伐謀，其次伐交，其次伐兵，其下攻城。攻城之法為不得已。修櫓轒轀]、具器械、三月而後成，距闉，又三月而後已。將不勝其忿，而蟻附之，殺士三分之一，而城不拔者，此攻之災也。故善用兵者，屈人之兵而非戰也。拔人之城而非攻也，破人之國而非久也，必以全爭于天下，故兵不頓，而利可全，此謀攻之法也。

故用兵之法，十則圍之，五則攻之，倍則分之，敵則能戰之，少則能逃之，不若則能避之。故小敵之堅，大敵之擒也。

*" Siege warfare should only be
undertaken if it is unavoidable.* **"**

Thus it follows that the highest form of warfare is to out-think
the enemy; next is to break his alliances; then to defeat his armies in
battle; the lowest form is to besiege his cities. Siege warfare should only
be undertaken if it is unavoidable. The time involved is too costly: it
takes up to three months to construct the various moveable shelters,
transports and other siege engines; it takes another three months to raise
earthworks against the walls. If the general loses patience and sends his
men swarming like ants around the city, it will cost him a third of his
army with no result. These are the disastrous pitfalls of a siege.

Thus a skilful general must defeat the enemy without coming to
battle, take his cities without a siege and overthrow his state without a
long campaign. He must make every effort under Heaven to achieve total
victory with his forces undiminished: this is the art of strategic offence.

Thus, when deploying your troops, if you outnumber the enemy
ten to one, surround him; five to one, attack him; two to one, split him.[7]
If forces are equal, engage him in open battle; if you in turn are slightly
outnumbered, evade his advances; if you are heavily outnumbered,
withdraw completely. A smaller force, no matter how determined, will
always succumb to a larger one.

---

[7] The terse and elliptical nature of classical Chinese means that there are many passages in the
text that are open to different interpretations. Sometimes, as here, the possible interpretations
are almost opposites. The phrase that I have translated as "split them [the enemy]" is taken by
some translators to mean "divide your own force in two", presumably so that you may attack from
both front and rear or front and flank. Classical Chinese is, however, a language of balanced
constructions, and, when in doubt, I have allowed the text itself to dictate my interpretation,
as it does here.

夫將者，國之輔也。輔周則國必強，輔隙則國必弱。故君之所以患于軍者三：不知軍之不可以進而謂之進，不知軍之不可 以退而謂之退，是為縻軍；不知三軍之事，而同三軍之政者，則軍士 惑矣；不知三軍之權，而同三軍之任，則軍士疑矣。三軍既惑且疑，則諸侯之難至矣，是謂亂軍引勝。

故知勝有五：知可以戰與不可以戰者勝，識眾寡之用者勝，上下同欲 者勝，以虞待不虞者勝，將能而君不御者勝。此五者，知勝之道也。

故曰：知己知彼，百戰不殆；不知彼而知己，一勝一負；不知彼不知 己，每戰必殆。

> **“** *...we may say that to know yourself and to know your enemy, you will gain victory a hundred times out of a hundred...* **”**

The army's commander is the mainstay of the State; if his support is solid, the State will be strong; if his support is flawed, the State will be weak. Indeed, there are three ways a ruler can bring disaster on his army. He may hobble the army by ordering advance or retreat at the wrong time; he may confuse his troops by interfering in military organization without understanding it; he may dishearten his troops by meddling with rank and responsibility without regard to the consequences. If they see the army confused and discomfited, the lesser lords and princes will take advantage and begin to cause trouble. This is called spurning victory by disrupting the army.

There are five keys to victory: knowing when to fight and when not to, brings victory; knowing what to do both when superior in numbers and when outnumbered, brings victory; holding officers and men united in purpose, brings victory; careful preparation to catch the enemy unprepared, brings victory; a skilful general given free rein by the ruler, brings victory. These five together are the true path to success.

Thus we may say that if you know yourself and know your enemy, you will gain victory a hundred times out of a hundred. If you know yourself but do not know your enemy you will meet one defeat for every victory. If you know neither yourself nor your enemy, you will never be victorious.

形篇

孫子曰：昔之善戰者，先為不可勝，以侍敵之可勝。不可勝在己，可 勝在敵。故善戰者，能為不可勝，不能使敵之必可勝。故曰：勝可知，而不可為。不可勝者，守也；可勝者，攻也。守則不足，攻則有餘。善守者，藏于九地之下；善攻者，動于九天之上。故能自保而全勝 也。

Deployment

> *"Whilst you are unsure of victory, defend..."*

The great generals of old first ensured that they themselves were beyond defeat and then waited for the enemy to make themselves vulnerable. Thus we can say that although you have it in your own hands to place yourself beyond defeat, you cannot, of yourself, bring about the defeat of the enemy. Whilst you are unsure of victory, defend; when you are sure of victory, attack. Defence should indicate that you are not in a position to defeat the enemy, attack that you are even stronger than you need to be. A skilled defender digs himself in deeper than the ninth level of the Earth; a skilled attacker falls on the enemy from above the ninth level of Heaven.[8] In this way you can both protect yourself completely and ensure total victory.

---

[8] The ultimate level of heaven in Buddhist mythology.

見勝不過眾人之所知,非善之善者也;戰勝而天下曰善,非善之善者也。故舉秋毫不為多力,見日月不為明目,聞雷霆不為聰耳。古之所謂善戰者,勝于易勝者也。故善戰之勝也,無智名,無勇功。故其戰 勝不忒。不忒者,其所措必勝,勝已敗者也。故善戰者,立于不敗之地,而不失敵之敗也。是故勝兵先勝而後求戰,敗兵先戰而後求勝。善用兵者,修道而保法,故能為勝敗之政。

兵法:一曰度,二曰量,三曰數,四曰稱,五曰勝。地生度,度生量,量生數,數生稱,稱生勝。故勝兵若以鎰稱銖,敗兵若以銖稱鎰。勝者之戰民也,若決積水于千仞之谿者,形也。

> *" Being prepared for all circumstances is what ensures certain victory...* "*

Only to see victory when it is already clear to all is by no means the height of excellence; a victory that is acclaimed by all and sundry is by no means the greatest of victories. It takes no great strength to lift a feather; you don't need keen eyesight to see the sun, nor keen ears to hear thunder. The great warriors of old not only won victories, but won them with ease; because their victories were achieved without apparent difficulty, they did not bring them great fame for their wisdom or respect for their courage. Being prepared for all circumstances is what ensures certain victory, for it means you are fighting an enemy who is already beaten. Thus a great soldier first places himself in an invincible position, and then ensures he does not miss the crucial opportunity to defeat the enemy. A successful army first ensures invincibility, and only then engages the enemy. A vanquished army will have gone into battle first, and only then looked for the means of victory. A great strategist follows his Moral Compass and adheres to his methods of Regulation, for these are the means by which he determines victory or defeat.

In the Art of War, first comes scoping, then measurement, then calculation, then balancing[9] and finally victory. The Earth is the basis for scoping, scoping the basis for measurement, measurement the basis for calculation, calculation the basis for balancing, and balancing the basis for victory. A victorious army is just as an yi is to a shu, and a defeated army is as a shu to an yi.[10] A victorious army carries all the weight of flood water plunging into a thousand-foot gorge.

---

[9] The translation of these four terms is, again, my own interpretation as any precise technical meaning for the original Chinese characters has been lost. What is clearly implied is a process from general to specific, or from broad-brush to fine detail.

[10] An yi is a unit of weight approximating to 500 grams and a shu is approximately 1 gram.

勢篇

孫子曰：凡治眾如治寡，分數是也；鬥眾如鬥寡，形名是也；三軍之 眾，可使必受敵而無敗，奇正是也；兵之所加，如以碫投卵者，虛實是也。

Momentum

"To hold an entire army unbroken in the face of an enemy attack is achieved by use of both the oblique and the direct."

The principles of control for a large force are the same as for a small one; the essential factor is how they are divided up. Deploying a large army in battle is just like deploying a small one; it is a matter of formation and communication. To hold an entire army unbroken in the face of enemy attack is achieved by use of both the oblique and the direct. To make the force of your army's attack like a grindstone crushing an egg, you must master the substantial and the insubstantial.[11]

---

[11] The following two chapters are crucial to understanding Sunzi's approach to war. He uses two pairs of terms "zheng" 正 and "qi" 奇, and "shi" 實 and "xu" 虛 which are very challenging to translate with the full weight of meaning the Chinese carries. Underlying both pairs is the understanding that apparent opposites are, in fact, part of the same continuum, and that in harnessing one aspect you are also automatically involving the other. Thus, in translating "shi" and "xu" as substantial and insubstantial, we should really understand them as that which appears to have substance or weight and that which appears not to. Equally with "zheng" and "qi" superficial appearances mask a different reality where it is the indirect that actually achieves the purpose whilst the direct merely holds a position or distracts attention. Since these terms are part of a continuum, their meanings may also be relative. Something that is insubstantial to the defender may in fact be substantial to the attacker, and something that appears direct to one army is in fact indirect to the one opposing it. To Sunzi, much of the art of skilled leadership lies in harnessing these paradoxes.

凡戰者，以正合，以奇勝。故善出奇者，無窮如天地，不竭如江河。終而復始，日月是也。死而復生，四時是也。聲不過五，五聲之變，不可勝聽也。色不過五，五色之變，不可勝觀也。味不過五，五味之變，不可勝嘗也。戰勢不過奇正，奇正之變，不可勝窮之也。奇正相生，如環之無端，孰能窮之？

激水之疾，至于漂石者，勢也；鷙鳥之疾，至于毀折者，節也。是故善戰者，其勢險，其節短。勢如張弩，節如發機。

In all kinds of warfare, the direct approach is used for attack, but the oblique is what achieves victory. A general who understands the use of the oblique has a source of tactics as inexhaustible as Heaven and Earth, which, like the Rivers and the Oceans, will never run dry. Like the Sun and Moon, they diminish and then replenish; they constantly renew themselves like the cycle of the Four Seasons. There are only five basic notes in music,[12] but their variations are infinite. There are only five primary colours,[13] but when blended, their shades and hues are limitless. There are only five principal tastes,[14] but their combinations produce more flavours than can ever be tasted. In military strategy, there is only the direct and the oblique, but between them they offer an inexhaustible range of tactics. The direct and the oblique lead naturally one into the other, like an ever-turning wheel, so who can ever exhaust their resource? The surge of rolling flood-water washes away boulders: this is called momentum. The swoop of a falcon strikes and kills its prey: this is called timing. Thus for a skilled warrior, his momentum must be irresistible and his timing precise. Momentum is the tension in a crossbow arm; timing is the pulling of the trigger.

> *"In military strategy, there is only the direct and the oblique, but between them they offer an inexhaustible range of tactics."*

---

[12] Ancient Chinese music worked with a pentatonic scale.

[13] Red, blue, yellow, black and white.

[14] Sweet, salty, sour, bitter and savouriness – the last is now known as "umami".

紛紛紜紜,鬥亂而不可亂也。渾渾沌沌,形圓而不可敗也。亂生于治,怯生于勇,弱生于強。治亂,數也;勇怯,勢也;強弱,形也。故善動敵者,形之,敵必從之;予之,敵必取之。以利動之,以卒動 之。

故善戰者,求之于勢,不責于人,故能擇人而任勢。任勢者,其戰人 也,如轉木石。木石之性,安則靜,危則動,方則止,圓則行。故善戰人之勢,如轉圓石于千仞之山者,勢也。

In the rolling turmoil of battle, your troops may appear to be in chaos, but in fact cannot be disordered; in tumult and confusion, your dispositions may seem formless, but in fact remain invincible. In this way, apparent confusion masks true organization; cowardice masks courage; weakness masks strength. Confusion and organization are a matter of deployment. Cowardice and courage are a matter of momentum. Strength and weakness are a matter of formation. A general skilled in out-manoeuvring the enemy uses formation to make them follow him; he offers a sacrifice to make them snatch at it; he lays bait to tempt them and sets his troops in ambush to wait for them.[15]

The skilled general seeks combined momentum and does not rely on individual prowess; he knows how to choose his men for maximum combined effect. This combined effect in battle has the power of rolling logs and boulders. It is the nature of logs and boulders to remain still on level ground, but to roll down a slope; they will come quickly to a halt if they have squared-off sides, but keep rolling if they are round. The momentum of skilled warriors is like a round boulder tumbling down a thousand-foot mountain. This is what I have to say on momentum.

---

[15] This paragraph is one of the most difficult to translate in the whole text. I offer my version as being in keeping both with the structure of the original Chinese and with the overall tenor of Sunzi's approach, but make no claim to it being definitive.

虛實篇

孫子曰：凡先處戰地而待敵者佚，後處戰地而趨戰者勞。

故善戰者，致人而不致于人。

能使敵自至者，利之也；能使敵不得至者，害之也。故敵佚能勞之，飽能飢之，安能動之。

出其所不趨，趨其所不意。行千里而不勞者，行于無人之地也。攻而 必取者，攻其所不守也。守而必固者，守其所不攻也。

The Substantial
and the Insubstantial

*" Attack at points which the enemy
must scramble to defend... "*

It is a general principle that the army which arrives first at the site of
battle and waits for the enemy will be fresh, and the army that arrives
second to the field and has to rush into battle will be laboured
and exhausted.

Thus a great warrior takes control of others and does not let others
control him.[16] By holding out temptation, he can make the enemy
approach; by inflicting harm, he can hold them at a distance. Using the
same principles, if the enemy are taking their ease, he can rouse them;
if they are well-provisioned, he can starve them; if they are encamped,
he can move them on. Attack at points which the enemy must scramble
to defend, and launch lightning attacks where they are not expected.
It is possible to march your army a thousand li as long as it is across
unoccupied territory. To be sure of success, only attack at undefended
areas. To be sure in defence, mount your defences at those places the
enemy cannot attack.

---

[16] Nowhere in the text is it more evident than here that Sunzi pre-supposes no other master of the
art of war exists who might be similarly advising the enemy.

故善攻者,敵不知其所守。善守者,敵不知其所 攻。

微乎微乎,至于無形,神乎神乎,至于無聲,故能 為敵之司命。

進而不可禦者,沖其虛也;退而不可追者,速而 不可及也。故我欲戰,敵雖高壘深溝,不得不與 我戰者,攻其所必救也;我不欲戰,雖畫 地而守之,敵不得與我戰者,乖其所之也。

故形人而我無形,則我專而敵分;我專為一,敵 分為十,是以十攻其 一也,則我眾而敵寡;能以 眾擊寡者,則吾之所與戰者,約矣。吾所 與戰之地不可知,不可知,則敵所備者多,敵所 備者多,則吾之所戰 者,寡矣。

*" To advance without the possibility
of being checked, you must strike fast at
the enemy's weakest points. "*

Thus when facing a warrior skilled in attack, the enemy does not know where to defend; with a warrior skilled in defence, they do not know where to attack. Be subtle! Be subtle! You can make yourself invisible. Be secretive! Be secretive! You can move without a sound. Thus you hold the enemy's fate in your hands. To advance without the possibility of being checked, you must strike fast at the enemy's weakest points. To retreat without the possibility of being caught, you must march at a speed the enemy cannot match. If you want to bring the enemy to battle, even though he is entrenched behind the deepest of ditches and highest of ramparts, you must attack at a point he cannot afford not to rally to.

If you do not wish to engage with the enemy, even though your defences are no more than a line in the ground, you can prevent them attacking by luring them away with a feint or a decoy. If you can see the enemy's dispositions, but they cannot see yours, then you can keep your forces united whilst they must split up to allow for all possibilities. If you are a single unit but the enemy is divided into ten, then the odds are ten to one in your favour at any given point. If you have a superior force you can use to attack an enemy's inferior one, then inevitably you outnumber them. If you can keep your point of attack secret from the enemy, then they will be forced to mount defences at many different places. With their forces thus stretched, wherever you attack it will be with superior numbers. If they reinforce their van, they weaken their rear; if they reinforce their left flank, they weaken their right and so on. If they try to reinforce every possible position, then every position will be weakened.

Weakness in numbers stems from having to mount defences; strength in numbers stems from forcing the enemy to mount such defences.

故備前則後寡,備後則前寡,故備左則右寡,備右則左寡,無所不備,則無所不寡。寡者備人者也,眾者使人備己者也。

故知戰之地,知戰之日,則可千里而會戰。不知戰之地,不知戰之日,則左不能救右,右不能救左,前不能救後,後不能救前,而況遠者 數十里,近者數里乎?

以吾度之,越人之兵雖多,亦奚益于勝敗哉?!

故曰:勝可為也。敵雖眾,可使無鬥。

故策之而知得失之計,作之而知動靜之理,形之而知死生之地,角之 而知有餘不足之處。

"*Lay plans to discover the enemy's intentions...*"

Thus if you know in advance the time and place of engagement, you can march a thousand li and still join battle. If you do not know the time and place of engagement, then you do not know whether to reinforce your van or your rear, your left or your right flank – imagine the difficulties if your furthest divisions are separated by tens of li, and even if the closest ones are only a few li apart.

By my calculations, the army of Yue[17] outnumbers ours, but this advantage will most surely not bring them victory!

I say that victory will be ours. Even if the enemy outnumber you, you can prevent them from joining battle.

Lay plans to discover the enemy's intentions and their likelihood of success; provoke him to understand the dynamics of his movement and inactivity; force him to deploy where you can study his formations so that you can see his strongpoints and weaknesses; take his measure so that you know where his dispositions are under-manned and where they are over-manned.

In deploying your troops, the greatest skill is in keeping the enemy in the dark. Keep your dispositions secret so that the most thorough of searches cannot discover them and they are hidden from the sharpest of intellects.

---

[17] On occasions Sunzi becomes specific rather than generalizing, and instances such as this one are taken as evidence that he was indeed writing for King He Lü of Wu. It is certainly true that the states of Wu and Yue were at war for a long period from the sixth to early fifth century BCE, culminating in fact in the defeat of Wu in 473 BCE.

故形兵之極, 至于無形; 無形, 則深間不能窺, 智者不能謀。

因形而錯勝于眾, 眾不能知; 人皆知我所以勝之形, 而莫知吾所以制 勝之形。故其戰勝不復, 而應形于無窮。

夫兵形象水, 水之形避高而趨下, 兵之形, 避實而擊虛, 水因地而制 流, 兵應敵而制勝。故兵無常勢, 水無常形, 能因敵變化而取勝者, 謂之神。

故五行無常勝, 四時無常位, 日有短長, 月有死生。

The common people cannot comprehend how I contrive my victories from the dispositions of the enemy themselves; all they see are the tactics by which victory is won, and none of them understand the planning behind them. Never employ the same strategy twice, but use the infinite variety at your disposal.

Military strategy is like water, which flows away from high ground towards low ground; so, in your tactics, avoid the enemy's strengths and attack his weaknesses. Water adapts its course according to the terrain; in the same way you should shape your victory around the enemy's dispositions. There are no constants in warfare, any more than water maintains a constant shape. Thus a general who gains victory by shaping his tactics according to the enemy ranks with the Immortals.

None of the Five Elements[18] remains dominant for long; none of the Four Seasons lasts indefinitely; the Sun rises and sets; the Moon waxes and wanes.

> **"***Military strategy is like water, which flows away from high ground to low ground...***"**

---

[18] The Five Elements of traditional Chinese medicine and philosophy: wood, water, earth, metal and fire.

軍爭篇

孫子曰：凡用兵之法，將受命于君，合軍聚眾，交和而舍，莫難于軍爭。軍爭之難者，以迂為直，以患為利。故迂其途，而誘之以利，後人發，先人至，此知迂直之計者也。

Manoeuvres
against the Enemy

*❝Manoeuvres against the enemy can
bring great advantage or great peril. ❞*

In the conduct of war, the general receives his orders from the ruler; it is then the general's job to marshal the forces available to him, put them into effective order and build their encampment. Then, most difficult of all, he commences his manoeuvres against the enemy. The inherent difficulties of this lie in the need to turn the devious into the direct, and to turn the disadvantageous into advantage. For example, he may lay a false trail away from his true objective, so tempting the enemy off course, and thus arrive at his real destination before the enemy, even though he sets out after him.[19] This shows mastery of the devious.

---

[19] This rather cumbersome sentence, whose meaning does not really seem to justify its complexity, is an excellent example of the challenges of translation. In the original it is two carefully balanced three-character phrases of great simplicity which offer almost no clue as to their specific meaning.

故軍爭為利, 軍爭為危。舉軍而爭利, 則不及;委軍而爭利, 則輜重捐。是故卷甲而趨, 日夜不處, 倍道兼行, 百里而爭利, 則擒三將軍, 勁者先, 疲者後, 其法十一而至;五十里而爭利, 則蹶上將軍, 其法半至;三十里而爭利, 則三分之二至。是故軍無輜重則亡, 無糧食則亡, 無委積則亡。

故不知諸侯之謀者, 不能豫交;不知山林、險阻、沮澤之形者, 不能行軍;不用鄉導者, 不能得地利。

> " *...a general must acquaint himself thoroughly with the terrain...before he can march his army through it.* "

Manoeuvres against the enemy can bring great advantage or great peril. If you wait to muster your force with full equipment before trying to seize an advantage, you risk arriving too late. If you rush out under-equipped to seize an advantage, you risk also losing the equipment you left behind.[20] Equally to be considered is that if you order the men on forced marches with their armour rolled in their packs, moving night and day without rest to double the distance covered, then a march of 100 li to seize an advantage will result in the capture of the commanders of all three divisions. The stronger men will surge ahead and the weaker ones fall to the rear, and only a tenth of your strength will actually reach the destination on time. If the march is 50 li, then the leader of the vanguard will be captured, and half your force will arrive. If you march only 30 li, then two-thirds will arrive. On the same principles, an army must have its baggage train, provisions and supply dumps, otherwise it is lost.

A ruler must understand the priorities of the local nobles before he can make profitable alliances; a general must acquaint himself thoroughly with the terrain – its mountains and forests, its halts and impasses, swamps and marshes – before he can march his army through it. He must use local knowledge to take best advantage of the natural features.

---

[20] Commentators all agree that the text at this point is corrupt; this translation is the sense most usually adopted.

故兵以詐立，以利動，以分和為變者也。

故其疾如風，其徐如林，侵掠如火，不動如山，難知如陰，動如雷震。掠鄉分眾，廓地分守，懸權而動。先知迂直之計者勝，此軍爭之法也。

軍政曰：「言不相聞，故為金鼓；視而不見，故為旌旗。」夫 金鼓旌旗者，所以一人之耳目也；人既專一，則勇者不得獨進，怯者不得獨退，此用眾之法也。故夜戰多火鼓，晝戰多旌旗，所以變人之耳目也。

In warfare, subterfuge is your foundation, advantage your motivation, and circumstance determines your formation. You must be swift as the wind, dense as the forest, rapacious as fire, steadfast like a mountain, mysterious as night and mighty as thunder. Organize your men in the plundering of the enemy's country, allocate captured land amongst them to their best advantage, and do not act without careful consideration. Victory belongs to him who has mastered the combination of the devious and the direct. Such is the art of manoeuvring against the enemy.

The Book of Military Management[21] says: in battle, the human voice is not strong enough to be heard which is why we use gongs and drums; our eyesight is not acute enough, which is why we use banners and flags.

Gongs and drums, and banners and flags make the army hear with the same ear and see with the same eye. Thus unified in understanding, the brave cannot advance alone nor the cowardly retreat. This is the art of troop management. In night warfare, make more use of signal fires and drums, and in daytime rely on banners and flags, thus adapting to the eyes and ears of your troops.

---

[21] Stylistically, Sunzi's chapter ends with his formulaic sentence: "Such is the art of manoeuvring against the enemy." It is not clear why he then appends an extract from another book, nor is anything further known about this work. It is possible that the text has been corrupted by the inclusion into the text of what was originally a commentary or comparison by a later author.

故三軍可奪氣，將軍可奪心。是故朝氣銳，晝氣惰，暮氣歸。故善用 兵者，避其銳氣，擊其惰歸，此治氣者也。以治待亂，以靜待嘩，此治心者也。以近待遠，以佚待勞，以飽待飢，此治力者也。無邀正正 之旗，無擊堂堂之陣，此治變者也。

故用兵之法，高陵勿向，背丘勿逆，佯北勿從，銳卒勿攻，餌兵勿食，歸師勿遏，圍師遺闕，窮寇勿迫，此用兵之法也。

" ...never attack uphill, nor defend downhill; do not be lured into attack by feigned flight... "

A whole army may become demoralized, and a general may lose heart. In the morning a soldier is full of fight, in the afternoon he is slowing down, and in the evening he thinks only of returning to camp. A skilled general will avoid the enemy when they are full of fight, and engage with them when their thoughts have turned to their beds. This is mastery of morale. He uses discipline in the face of disorder, and calmness to confront frenzy. This is mastery of emotion. To be close to the battlefield whilst the enemy is still far away, to be fresh and rested when the enemy is exhausted, to be well-fed when the enemy is hungry, this is mastery of the upper hand. Holding off from an enemy whose banners are well ordered, and not engaging with an army in tight formation, this is mastery of circumstance.

Here are some of the basic principles of war: never attack uphill, nor defend downhill; do not be lured into attack by feigned flight, and do not attack an enemy who is rested and full of fight. Do not swallow the bait put out for you, and do not get in the way of an army that is homeward bound. When you surround an enemy, always leave them a way out, and do not press a cornered foe too hard.[22] This is the art of waging war.

---

[22] These last three pieces of advice seem uncharacteristically soft on the enemy, but they should be understood not as letting the enemy get away, rather as denying them the savage courage that comes from desperation.

九變篇

孫子曰：凡用兵之法，將受命于君，合軍聚衆，圮地無舍，衢地交和，絕地勿留，圍地則謀，死地則戰。

途有所不由，軍有所不擊，城有所不攻，地有所不爭，君命有所不受。

故將通于九變之利者，知用兵矣；將不通于九變之利，雖知地形，不能得地之利矣；治兵不知九變之朮，雖知五利，不能得人之用矣。

The Nine Variables [23]

*" There will be roads that should
not be followed; there will be armies
that should not be attacked... "*

In the conduct of war, the general receives his orders from the
ruler; it is then the general's job to marshal the forces available to
him. If the terrain is unfavourable, do not encamp; if roads and
communications are good, make sure of your allies; do not linger in
difficult ground; if you are surrounded, find a way out by stratagem; in
a life-or-death situation, fight head-on. There will be roads that should
not be followed; there will be armies that should not be attacked; there
will be cities that should not be besieged; there will be positions that
should not be fought over; there will even be orders from your ruler that
should not be followed. [24] A general who thoroughly understands the
Nine Variables will know how to use his armies. A general who does not
thoroughly understand them, however well he knows the lie of the land,
will not be able to turn it to his advantage. A commander may be well
acquainted with the Five Advantages, [25] but, without understanding of the
Nine Variables, he will never use his men to their best effect.

---

[23] Sunzi does not in fact list nine variables. Some commentators suggest that "nine" simply means
a very large number, which seems improbable on a number of counts. Given the shortness of the
chapter, it is perhaps more likely that the text is corrupt and a portion is missing.

[24] This is Sunzi at his most pragmatic – and daring. In any circumstances apart from war, loyalty
and obedience to your ruler should be paramount.

[25] Another argument for corruption of the text in this chapter since these are not defined,
whereas a few lines later, the five pitfalls that may ensnare a general are carefully described.

49

是故智者之慮, 必雜于利害。雜于利, 而務可信也; 雜于害, 而患可 解也。

是故屈諸侯者以害, 役諸侯者以業, 趨諸侯者以利。

故用兵之法, 無恃其不來, 恃吾有以待也; 無恃其不攻, 恃吾有所不 可攻也。

故將有五危: 必死, 可殺也; 必生, 可虜也; 忿速, 可侮也; 廉潔, 可辱也; 愛民, 可煩也。凡此五者, 將之過也, 用兵之災也。覆軍殺將, 必以五危, 不可不察也。

"A wise leader always considers both advantages and disadvantages equally."

A wise leader always considers both advantages and disadvantages equally. By pausing to consider the disadvantages of an advantageous situation, he can be sure of achieving his aims; by considering the potential advantages of a perilous situation, he can find a way of resolving his difficulties. Keep the other lords and princes in their place by harrying them; worry them and keep them busy; lead them on with the hope of some advantage.

In waging war, do not rely on the enemy not arriving to battle but on your own readiness to receive them; do not rely on them not attacking, rather be sure of the defensibility of your own position.

There are five pitfalls that may ensnare a general: reckless disregard for death will indeed result in death; too much regard for life will result in capture; a quick temper can be provoked into rash action; a misplaced sense of honour brings only shame; over-solicitude for the men just causes needless trouble and anxiety. These five are the common failings of generals and are disastrous in their effect on the successful conduct of war. When an army is defeated and its general slain, look no further than these five for the cause. They demand study.

行軍篇

孫子曰：凡處軍、相敵，絕山依谷，視生處高，戰隆無登，此處山之　軍也。

絕水必遠水；客絕水而來，勿迎之于水內，令半濟而擊之，利；欲戰者，無附于水而迎客；視生處高，無迎水流，此處水上之軍也。

絕斥澤，惟亟去無留；若交軍于斥澤之中，必依水草，而背眾樹，此處斥澤之軍也。

平陸處易，而右背高，前死後生，此處平陸之軍也。

On the March

" *...choose an elevated spot for your
camp facing east...* "

In the matter of siting your own camp and observing the movements
of the enemy, pass by the mountains and stay within the valleys,
but choose an elevated spot for your camp facing east. Never climb
to join battle on high ground. That is what you need to know about
mountain terrain.

Once you have crossed a river, move well away from it. If the enemy
crosses a river offering combat, never try to meet them mid-stream; you
can seize the advantage by letting half their force across and
then attacking. However eager you are for battle, do not attack the
enemy as they approach a river; choose an elevated spot facing east to
wait for them, and never attack upstream. This is how to fight
around rivers.

Cross salt-marshes as quickly as possible and do not linger. If you
come to battle in such marshes, fight in the water-meadows with trees at
your back. This is how to fight in salt-marshes.

On level ground where it is easy to set up camp, chose a spot with
high ground to your right and rear so that the danger is in front of you
and safety behind. So much for fighting on level ground.

凡此四軍之利，黃帝之所以勝四帝也。

凡軍好高而惡下，貴陽而賤陰，養生而處實，軍無百疾，是謂必勝。

丘陵堤防，必處其陽，而右背之。此兵之利，地之助也。上雨，水沫至，欲涉者，待其定也。凡地有絕澗、天井、天牢、天羅、天陷、天隙，必亟去之，勿近也。吾遠之，敵近之；吾迎之，敵背之。軍旁有險阻、潢井、葭葦、林木、蘙薈者，必謹慎復索之，此伏奸之 所處也。

It was through knowing how to use these four types of terrain to advantage that the Yellow Emperor was able to vanquish the Four Emperors.[26]

All armies love the high ground and hate the low, and prefer sunny places to dark and shade. If you look after the health of your men and camp on firm dry ground, your army will avoid all the usual diseases. This is a sure recipe for victory.

When you come to hills or man-made banks, take up position on the sunny side with the high ground to your right and rear. This will deploy your men to their best advantage, and make full use of the terrain. If a river is swollen with rain-water and you wish to cross it, wait until it subsides. If you encounter mountain cascades, deep hollows, dead ends, deep undergrowth, swamps or narrow ravines, keep well clear of them and stay away. At the same time try to force the enemy towards such places, so that you are facing them and they have them to their rear. If the army is passing through hilly ground where there may be ponds with reed beds or woods with thickets, these must be thoroughly searched for they are ideal cover for spies and traitors.

---

[26] The Yellow Emperor was one of the legendary rulers of Chinese mythological history, accepted as a real figure at this time. There is, however, no surviving story of him conquering four other emperors. We must presume it was lost over the centuries.

敵近而靜者,恃其險也;遠而挑戰者,欲人之進也;其所居易者,利 也。

眾樹動者,來也;眾草多障者,疑也;鳥起者,伏也;獸駭者,覆也;塵高而銳者,車來也;卑而廣者,徒來也;散而條達者,樵采也;少而往來者,營軍也。

辭卑而備者,進也;辭強而進驅者,退也;輕車先出其側者,陣也.

If the enemy are close at hand but holding back from attack then they are confident in the strength of their position. If the enemy are far off but seem to be challenging you to battle, then they are trying to lure you in close. If their encampment seems open to attack, then it is a trap. If trees and bushes seem to be moving, the enemy is advancing. If you see unusual clumps among the reeds and grasses, the enemy is laying some kind of trap. If birds suddenly rise in their flight, there is an ambush[27] and startled animals mark a surprise attack. If dust rises high and distinct in the air, it is a sign of chariots; if the dust stays low but spreads out, it has been caused by infantry. When the dust separates along several different paths, the enemy are out collecting firewood. Small clouds of dust moving to and fro mean the enemy is pitching camp. If the enemy's heralds are conciliatory while the army still makes ready, then they are going to advance. If the heralds are haughty and the army looks ready to attack, they are preparing to retreat. If their chariots sally out and take up position on the flanks, the enemy is forming up for battle.

> **"***If their encampment seems open to attack, then it is a trap.***"**

---

[27] This does not mean birds rising from cover when disturbed by the enemy taking up position for an ambush. More subtly it means that birds in flight will deviate upwards from their course when flying over concealed men.

無約而請和者,謀也;奔走而陳兵者,期也;半進半退者,誘也。

杖而立者,飢也;汲而先飲者,渴也;見利而不進者,勞也;鳥集者,虛也;夜呼者,恐也;軍擾者,將不重也;旌旗動者,亂也;吏怒者,倦也;粟馬肉食,軍無懸缻而不返其舍者,窮寇也;諄諄翕翕,徐與人言者,失眾也.

數賞者,窘也;數罰者,困也;先暴而後畏其眾者,不精之至也;來委謝者,欲休息也。兵怒而相迎,久而不合,又不相去,必謹察之。

兵非貴益多也,惟無武進,足以并力、料敵、取人而已。

Offers of a truce with no solid commitments only indicate some kind of plot. If you see their troops rushing about and forming up, a decisive attack is coming. If the enemy seem to be half advancing and half retreating, it is a trap. If the soldiers are leaning on their spears, they are hungry; if those sent to draw water drink before they bring it back, the whole army is thirsty. If the enemy don't avail themselves of a clear opportunity, then they are exhausted. A place where birds gather undisturbed is unoccupied. Disturbance in camp at night means the enemy is fretful. Widespread unrest indicates weakness in the command. If the flags and banners begin to move around, there is disorder amongst the troops. If the officers seem angry and irritable, exhaustion is setting in. If the enemy are feeding grain to their horses and slaughtering their animals for meat, if they no longer hang up their cooking pots and return to their tents, then they are readying themselves for the final onslaught. Clusters of men whispering together are a sign of disaffection in the ranks. [28]

If rewards are being offered too freely, the enemy's resources are severely depleted. If punishment is being meted out too freely, the enemy is in dire straits. For the enemy general to start by being overbearing to his troops but end in fear of them is the height of stupidity. If their heralds come speaking soft and conciliatory words, they want a truce. If their troops come out in anger and form up opposite you for a long time without either engaging or retreating, be especially on your guard. If you hold no advantage in troop numbers, there is a military stalemate, and all you should do is concentrate your forces in one place, keep watch on the enemy and raise more troops.

---

[28] In this paragraph Sunzi shows himself to be not just a master of tactics but also of behavioural psychology.

夫惟無慮而 易敵者,必擒于人。卒未親附而罰之,則不服,不服則難用也。卒已親附而罰不行,則不 可用也。故令之以文,齊之以武,是謂必取。令素行以教其民,則民 服;令素不行以教其民,則民不服。令素行者,與眾相得也。

A general who recklessly underestimates the enemy is sure to be captured. A general who punishes his troops before he has won them over, will never be accepted by them and they will be useless to him. If he has already won them over but does not punish them when appropriate, they will still be useless. So you must bring your troops together with humane treatment, and bind them with discipline – this is the path to invincibility. Enact consistency in orders and instruction and the men will be loyal to you; if there is no consistency, they will not. It is of mutual benefit to general and men to maintain this consistency.

> **"** *A general who recklessly underestimates the enemy is sure to be captured.* **"**

地形篇

孫子曰：地形有通者、有挂者、有支者、有隘者、有險者、有遠者。

我可以往，彼可以來，曰通。通形者，先居高陽，利糧道，以戰則利。可以往，難以返，曰挂。挂形者，敵無備，出而勝之，敵若有備，出而不勝，則難以返，不利。我出而不利，彼出而不利，曰支。支形者，敵雖利我，我無出也，引而去之，令敵半出而擊之，利。

Terrain

" Passable ground is terrain that can be crossed by either side. "

Terrain may be classified thus: passable ground, entangling ground, neutral ground, narrow passes, rugged cliffs, and separating ground.

Passable ground is terrain that can be crossed by either side. To keep the upper hand in this kind of ground, make sure that it is you who occupy the sunny heights, and look to your supply lines. Entangling ground is such that although easy to sally forth from it is hard to re-occupy. On such ground, if the enemy is poorly prepared it is easy for you venture out and defeat them. If, however, the enemy is well prepared and your attack fails, it will be difficult for you to return and you will be at a severe disadvantage. If neither side can gain the upper hand by taking the initiative, that is called neutral ground. In this kind of terrain, even though the enemy may offer me a tempting advantage, I would restrain myself and draw the enemy out. Then, when his army is half-committed, I would be able to attack with the certainty of gaining the upper hand.

隘形者，我先居之，必盈之以待敵。若敵先居之，盈而勿從，不盈而從之。險形者，我先居之，必居高陽以待敵；若敵先居之，引而去之，勿從也。遠形者，勢均，難以挑戰，戰而不利。凡此六者，地之道也，將　之至任，不可不察也。

故兵有走者、有馳者、有陷者、有崩者、有亂者、有北者。凡此六者，非天之災，將之過也。夫勢均，以一擊十，曰走。卒強吏弱，曰馳。吏強卒弱，曰陷。大吏怒而不服，遇敵懟而自戰，將不知其能，曰崩。將弱不嚴，教道不明，吏卒無常，陳兵縱橫，曰亂。將不能料敵，以少合眾，以弱擊強，兵無選鋒，曰北。凡此六者，敗之道也，將　之至任，不可不察也。

As for narrow passes, I make sure I occupy and fortify them first, then wait for the enemy to enter. If the enemy gets there first, and he has had a chance to fortify the position, then do not follow him in. If, however, the pass is unfortified, you should follow and attack. Amongst rugged cliffs, if I get there first, I occupy the sunny heights and wait for the enemy. If they get there first, I restrain myself and try to draw them out. If you are in separating ground, and the two sides are evenly matched, it is difficult to come to battle and even if you do, you will gain no advantage. These are the six principles of terrain and it is a prime responsibility of any general thoroughly to understand them.

There are six degrees of misfortune which can befall an army, none of which stem from natural causes but all of which are the fault of the general. They are: flight, insubordination, decline, collapse, chaos and rout. Flight results when, on otherwise equal terms, one force attempts to attack another ten times its size. Insubordination results when the rank and file soldiers are strong but the officers weak. If the officers are strong and over-bearing and the rank and file too passive, the result is decline. Collapse occurs when the senior officers forget their responsibilities and take personal affront at the enemy. They will then attack on their own account before the general has been able to assess the chances of success. If the general is weak and does not enforce discipline; if his orders are not clear; if there is no consistency for officers and men and organization is haphazard, all this results in chaos. When the general is unable to make an accurate assessment of the strength of the enemy, he will end up pitching a small detachment against a larger one, or a weak one against a strong one, without putting his crack troops in the vanguard. The result is rout. These are the six paths to defeat and it is a prime responsibility of any general thoroughly to understand them.

夫地形者,兵之助也。料敵制勝,計險厄遠近,上將之道也。知此而n用戰者必勝;不知此而用戰者必敗。故戰道必勝,主曰無戰,必戰可也;戰道不勝,主曰必戰,無戰可也。故進不求名,退不避罪,惟人是保,而利合于主,國之寶也。

視卒如嬰兒,故可以與之赴深谿;視卒如愛子,故可與之俱死。厚而 不能使,愛而不能令,亂而不能治,譬若驕子,不可用也。

> *"The natural characteristics of the terrain are a soldier's friend."*

The natural characteristics of the terrain are a soldier's friend. An ability to assess the enemy and control the chances of victory, to calculate obstacles, dangers and distances: these are what make a great general. If he understands all this and puts it into practice, he is certain of victory. If he neither understands nor practises it, he will be defeated. If all these indications point to certain victory, then a general must fight, even if his ruler orders him not to. Equally he must defy his ruler's order's to fight if the signs do not point to victory. A general who advances without thought of personal glory, and retreats without a care for disgrace, who thinks only of protecting the people and benefitting his ruler – such a man is a treasure beyond price to his country.

If you treat your soldiers like your children, you can lead them into the deepest darkest places; if you see them as your beloved sons, they will stand by you to the death. If, however, you are too soft and do not establish firm leadership, too kindly and do not enforce your orders, if you are lax in your organization and cannot keep control – then your troops will be as useless to you as spoilt children.

知吾卒之可以擊, 而不知敵之不可擊, 勝之半也; 知敵之可擊, 而不 知吾卒之不可以擊, 勝之半也; 知敵之可擊, 知吾卒之可以擊, 而不 知地形之不可以戰, 勝之半也。 故知兵者, 動而不迷, 舉而不窮。 故曰: 知己知彼, 勝乃不殆; 知天知地, 勝乃可全。

These situations are only half-measures towards victory: knowing your own troops are prepared to attack, but not knowing the preparedness of the enemy; knowing the state of the enemy, but not of your own troops; knowing the readiness of both the enemy and your own troops, but not knowing the nature of the terrain. Thus also the experienced soldier only makes a move when he is sure of his direction and only takes to the road when he is sure of his supplies. This is why it is truly said: if you know the enemy and know yourself, you are sure of victory. If you know Heaven and Earth, your victory will be complete.

" *...the experienced soldier only makes a move when he is sure of his direction...* "

九地篇

孫子曰：用兵之法，有散地，有輕地，有爭地，有交地，有衢地，有重地，有圮地，有圍地，有死地。諸侯自戰其地，為散地。入人之地 不深者，為輕地。我得則利，彼得亦利者，為爭地。我可以往，彼可以來者，為交地。諸侯之地三屬，先至而得天下眾者，為衢地。入人 之地深，背城邑多者，為重地。山林、險阻、沮澤，凡難行之道者，為圮地。所從由入者隘，所從歸者迂，彼寡可以擊我之眾者，為圍地。疾戰則存，不疾戰則亡者，為死地。

The Nine Types of Ground

In military terms there is dispersing ground, slight ground, contentious ground, open ground, linking ground, significant ground, difficult ground, constricted ground and desperate ground.[29] If a local ruler is fighting in his own territory, that is dispersing ground. If you have advanced only a short way into enemy territory, that is slight ground. Territory that is of equal benefit to both sides is contentious ground. If territory provides access and egress to both sides, it is open ground. Linking ground has borders with three different states, so that whoever controls it controls the bulk of the Empire. If you are deep in enemy territory, with many captured and garrisoned cities behind you, you are in significant ground. Forested mountains, rugged cliffs, marshes and wetlands – all territory that is hard to cross – is difficult ground. Territory with narrow access from which there is no direct retreat, so that a small force can easily defeat a large one, is called constricted ground. If you have to fight for your life and the least delay spells disaster, that is desperate ground.

---

[29] It has to be admitted that the translation of the names for each type of ground is fairly arbitrary since even in the original, the words take their meaning from their definitions rather than have a clear meaning in their own right. Other translators offer different versions, all equally acceptable.

是故散地則無戰，輕地則無止，爭地則無攻，衢地則合交，重地則掠，圮地則行，圍地則謀，死地則戰。所謂古之善用兵者，能使敵人前後不相及，眾寡不相恃，貴賤不相救，上下不相收，卒離而不集，兵合而不齊。合于利而動，不合于利而止。

敢問："敵眾整而將來，待之若何？"曰："先奪其所愛，則聽矣。"

兵之情主速，乘人之不及，由不虞之道，攻其所不戒也。

So, do not fight on dispersing ground and do not halt on slight ground. Do not attack on contentious ground and maintain your communications on open ground. Form alliances on linking ground and take the opportunity to plunder significant ground. Keep marching through difficult ground and use cunning when on constricted ground. On desperate ground, you fight. The great soldiers of old could separate the enemy's van from their rear, could prevent their small detachments and main force working together, stop the crack troops from helping the lesser divisions and disrupt communications between officers and subordinates. They could scatter the enemy and stop them from re-uniting, or keep them in confusion if they did manage to regroup. They would advance if it was advantageous or hold their position if it was not.

The question may be asked: what if the enemy advances to the attack with a large, well-organized army? My answer is: seize something they value highly, then they will listen to you.

The essence of military operations is speed. Take advantage of the enemy being unprepared; march by unexpected routes, and attack where they are not fortified against you.

" The essence of military operations is speed. "

凡為客之道：深入則專，主人不克。掠于饒野，
三軍足食。謹養而勿 勞，并氣積力，運并計謀，
為不可測。

投之無所往，死且不北。死焉
不得，士人盡力。兵士甚陷則不懼，無所往則
固，深入則拘，不得已 則鬥。

是故其兵不修而戒，不求而得，不約而親，不令
而信。

禁祥去 疑，至死無所之。

> *" Do not be afraid to send your troops into a position where there is no retreat... "*

The principles for campaigning in enemy territory are as follows: the deeper you penetrate, the greater the feeling of solidarity amongst your own troops, making it even more difficult for the enemy to withstand them. If you find yourself in fertile terrain, then forage enough supplies for your whole army. Look to the well-being of your soldiers and do not over-work them. Keep up their spirits and conserve their energy. Unite your forces with ingenious tactics and keep the enemy off-balance.

Do not be afraid to send your troops into a position from which there is no retreat, for they will prefer death to flight. If they can look death in the face and not flinch, then there is nothing that will be beyond them: both officers and men will exert themselves to the utmost. Soldiers of whatever rank lose their fear in dangerous circumstances; they stand firm when there is no retreat; deep in hostile territory, they show a united front; when there is no alternative, they will fight to the last.

Such soldiers will always be on their guard without your prompting; they will achieve your goals without your having to ask; they will be loyal without inducement and can be trusted to act correctly even without orders.

Ban all omen-taking and superstitious practices so that death is all they have to worry about.

吾士無餘財，非惡貨也；無餘命，非惡壽也。令發之日，士卒坐者涕沾襟，偃臥者淚交頤。投之無所往者，諸、劌之勇也。

故善用兵者，譬如率然。率然者，常山之蛇也。擊其首則尾至，擊其尾則首至，擊其中則首尾俱至。敢問："兵可使如率然乎？"曰："可。"夫吳人與越人相惡也，當其同舟而濟，遇風，其相救也，如左右手。

是故方馬埋輪，未足恃也。齊勇如一，政之道也.

剛柔皆得，地之理也。
故善用兵者，攜手若使一人，不得已也。

Soldiers are not poor because they despise wealth, nor short-lived because they disdain long life. On the day of battle, their cheeks and their tunics will be wet with tears, but once they are at the point of no return, they will show the courage of Zhuan Zhu and the bravery of Cao Gui.[30]

The skilled soldier should follow the example of the Shuai-Ran[31] – the famous snake of Chang Shan: if you attack its head, it strikes with its tail; if you attack its tail, it strikes with its head; and if you attack its body, it strikes with both head and tail. You ask me if an army can imitate the Shuai-Ran? I say it can! Although the people of Wu and Yue hate each other, if two of them are in the same boat, caught in a storm, they will help each other just as the left hand helps the right.

You cannot rely merely on tethering the horses and burying chariot wheels to hold onto your troops; the way to manage them properly is to unite them in courage.

Intelligent use of the terrain is the way to get the best out of both your strongest and your weakest men.

The skilled general leads his troops by the hand as though they were a single soldier, and they cannot help but follow.

---

[30] In 515 BCE, Zhuan Zhu was employed by Prince Guang of Wu (later to become King He Lü) to assassinate the then ruler King Liao. He succeeded in doing so with a dagger concealed inside a fish, but was immediately himself killed. Cao Gui was a courtier of the state of Lu, which, in 661 BCE, was about to surrender a large portion of territory to the state of Qi after a series of defeats. As the Duke of Qi stood at the altar about to receive the surrender, Cao Gui seized him, held a knife to his throat and demanded that he return the territory to Lu. In fear of his life, the Duke agreed and Cao Gui calmly stepped back to his place among the other courtiers. The Duke's advisers told the Duke he could not lose face by reneging on this new agreement or by punishing Cao Gui.

[31] No-one has ventured a positive identification of this snake.

將軍之事：靜以幽，正以治。能愚士卒之耳目，使之無知。易其事，革其謀，使人無識。易其居，迁其途，使人不得慮。帥與之期，如登高而去其梯。帥與之深入諸侯之地，而發其機，焚舟破釜，若驅群羊。驅而往，驅而來，莫知所之。聚三軍之眾，投之于險，此謂將軍之事也。九地之變，屈伸之力，人情之理，不可不察也。

凡為客之道：深則專，淺則散。去國越境而師者，絕地也；四達者，衢地也；入深者，重地也；入淺者，輕地也；背固前隘者，圍地也；無所往者，死地也。

It is the business of a general to keep tight-lipped to preserve secrecy; to be even-handed to ensure control; he must use tricks and rumours to keep both officers and men in the dark as to his true intentions. He should change his dispositions and plans, so no-one knows what he is up to. He should change his camp, and make detours so that his movements cannot be anticipated. When the time is ripe, a general should act like a man who climbs to a great height and then kicks away his ladder. He should plunge his army deep into enemy territory before he pulls the trigger. He is like a shepherd herding his flock to and fro so that no-one knows where he is really going. Marshalling his forces and leading them into danger is the business of a general. Adapting tactics to the Nine Types of Ground, assessing the merits of attack or retreat, understanding human nature – these are what demand a general's study.

When invading, the deeper you penetrate the better for holding your army together; if you stay too close to your own borders they will scatter. When you lead your troops across the border out of your own state, you are on difficult ground. If the terrain is accessible from all four directions, it is open ground. If you are deep into enemy territory, it is significant ground. If you are only a short way in, it is slight ground. If the enemy are entrenched behind you, and there are narrow passes ahead of you, it is constricted ground. When you have no way to turn, it is desperate ground.

" When you have no way to turn, it is desperate ground. "

是故散地,吾將一其志;輕地,吾將使之屬;爭地,吾將趨其後;交 地,吾將謹其守;衢地,吾將固其結;重地,吾將繼其食;圮地,吾 將進其途;圍地,吾將塞其闕;死地,吾將示之以不活。故兵之情:圍則御,不得已則鬥,過則從。

是故不知諸侯之謀者,不能預交。不知山林、險阻、沮澤之形者,不 能行軍。不用鄉導,不能得地利。四五者,不知一,非霸、王之兵也。夫霸、王之兵,伐大國,則其眾不得聚;威加于敵,則其交不得合。是故不爭天下之交,不養天下之權,信己之私,威加于敵,則其城 可拔,其國可隳。施無法之賞,懸無政之令,犯三軍之眾,若使一人。犯之以事,勿告以言。犯之以利,勿告以害。

" ...it is the soldier's nature to
fight back when he is surrounded, to
struggle when he thinks all is lost..."

On dispersing ground, I bind my men with a common purpose.
On slight ground, I keep my army in close formation. On contentious
ground, I bring up my rearguard. On open ground, I look to my
defences. On linking ground, I strengthen my alliances. On significant
ground, I protect my supply chain. On difficult ground, I press forward
on the route. On constricted ground, I block all the access points and
exits. On desperate ground, I show my troops the only choice left them
is between life and death. For, you must understand, it is the soldier's
nature to fight back when surrounded, to struggle when he thinks all is
lost, and to obey orders when in peril.

A leader must understand the priorities of the local nobles before
he can make profitable alliances; he must acquaint himself thoroughly
with the terrain – its mountains and forests, its halts and impasses,
swamps and marshes – before he can march his army through it. He
must use local knowledge to take best advantage of the natural features.
If he does not understand even one of the basic principles of war, he
is not a worthy general for his sovereign. A worthy general, when he
attacks a powerful state, does not allow the enemy to concentrate his
forces. He looms over them and prevents their allies from joining them.
He does not strive to form alliances all over the place, nor does he look
to bolster the power of other states. He keeps his own counsel, looming
threateningly over the enemy. Thus he is able to capture their cities
and conquer their kingdoms. Do not be bound by convention, but give
rewards as they are merited, and issue orders according to the situation.
Treat every man in your army exactly the same. Do not ask them simply
to trust your word, show them with your actions. It serves no purpose to
tell them if they are in danger.

投之亡地然後存,陷之死地然後生。夫眾陷于害,然後能為勝敗。

故為兵之事,在于佯順敵之意,并敵一向,千里殺將,是謂巧能成事 者也。

是故政舉之日,夷關折符,無通其使;勵于廊廟之上,以誅其事。敵人開闔,必亟入之,先其所愛,微與之期。踐墨隨敵,以決戰事。是 故始如處女,敵人開戶,後如脫兔,敵不及拒。

"In carrying out your military operations, give the impression of being sucked into the enemy's plans..."

You can lead them into the most desperate of situations confident that they will survive, for victory is to be plucked from defeat when they are in the greatest danger.

In carrying out your military operations, give the appearance of being sucked into the enemy's plans whilst actually targeting their exposed flank. In this way even 1000 li won't save their general from your sword. This is how you use skill and cunning to achieve your aims.

On the day war is declared, close off the passes, cancel the command-tallies[32] and cease all communications with the enemy's ambassadors. Consider your plans carefully in the temple and make your preparations. If the enemy leaves you an opening, rush through it. Seize what they hold most dear, and constrain them as to time. Modify your plans according to the enemy's movements until you can bring him to the crucial battle. Start off as coy as a virgin until the enemy opens the door to you, then move with the speed of a hare so they have no chance to resist.

---

[32] Various forms of tallies – bronze animal figures, wood or bamboo tablets which could be split into matching halves – were used as symbols of rank and authority, as ways of confirming authenticity of orders and as passports.

火攻篇

孫子曰：凡火攻有五：一曰火人，二曰火積，三曰火輜，四曰火庫，五曰火隊。

行火必有因，煙火必素具。發火有時，起火有日。時者，天之燥也。日者，月在其、壁、翼、軫也。凡此四宿者，風起之日也。

Attacking with Fire

" You need specific materials to make a fire attack... **"**

There are five ways of attacking the enemy with fire. The first is to burn the troops themselves; the second is to burn their stores; the third is to burn their equipment; the fourth to burn their arsenals, and the fifth to use fire arrows.

You need specific materials to make a fire attack, and these should be prepared in advance. There are also an appropriate season and appropriate days for raising such an attack. The proper season is when the weather is dry, and the suitable days are when the Moon is in the constellations of the Sieve, the Wing, the Wall or the Cross-bar. These are all days when the wind will blow.

凡火攻，必因五火之變而應之。火發于內，則早應之于外。火發而其 兵靜者，待而勿攻。極其火力，可從而從之，不可從而止。火可發于 外，無待于內，以時發之。火發上風，無攻下風。晝風久，夜風止。凡軍必知有五火之變，以數守之。

故以火佐攻者明，以水佐攻者強。水可以絕，不可以奪。

"A general who attacks with fire is demonstrating his intelligence..."

When mounting a fire attack, you must be prepared for five eventualities. If fire breaks out in the enemy's camp, be ready to make a swift attack. If however fire has broken out but the enemy are not panicked by it, then hold off your attack. Wait until the conflagration is at its height, take a view on whether it is practical to attack or not and act accordingly. If it is possible, set fires towards the enemy from outside their camp, don't wait to try to start fires inside, but seize the opportunity outside.

Remember to position yourself upwind of the fire you start, and never attack downwind of a fire. A wind that has blown for a long time during the day is likely to drop at night. Any army should be familiar with the five eventualities of a fire attack, and be prepared accordingly.

A general who attacks with fire is demonstrating his intelligence; one who uses water is simply showing his strength. Water can cut off an enemy, but it cannot despoil him of his equipment and supplies.[33]

---

[33] The inclusion of this brief comment on the use of water is puzzling in its lack of any detail or explanation. It is hard to see why Sunzi includes it as it adds nothing to the over all treatise. It may be supposed that the opportunities for serious attack using water were few and far between, and so there was little need to discuss them.

夫戰勝攻取，而不修其功者凶，命曰“費留”。故曰：明主慮之，良將修之。非利不動，非得不用，非危不戰。主不可以怒而興師，將不可以慍而致戰。合于利而動，不合于利而止。怒可以復喜，慍可以復悅，亡國不可以復存，死者不可以復生。故明君慎之，良將警之。此安國全軍之道也。

It is disastrous not to consolidate your achievements if you are victorious in battle and successful in your attacks – this is called waste and delay. Hence it is truly said that a wise ruler thinks ahead, and a good general builds on his victories. Do not move unless you see a clear advantage. Do not use your soldiers unless there is something to be gained. Do not fight if you are not in danger. A ruler should not call his general to arms simply out of anger; a general should not attack because he has been insulted. Only advance if it is to your clear advantage, otherwise stay put. Anger may change to contentment and insult to pleasure, but a kingdom once destroyed cannot be recovered, and the dead cannot be brought back to life. Thus a wise ruler is cautious, and a good general alert. This is the way to keep a country at peace and its armies intact.

> **"** *A ruler should not call his general to arms simply out of anger...* **"**

用間篇

孫子曰：凡興師十萬，出征千里，百姓之費，公家之奉，日費千金。內外騷動，怠于道路，不得操事者，七十萬家。

相守數年，以爭一日之勝，而愛爵祿百金，不知敵之情者，不仁之至也。非人之將也，非主之佐也，非勝之主也。故明君賢將，所以動而勝人，成功出于眾者，先知也。先知者，不可取于鬼神，不可象于事，不可驗于度。必取于人，知敵之情者也。

Using Spies[34]

> **"** *...foreknowledge cannot be found by consulting the spirits...* **"**

When you levy an army 100,000 strong and set out on a campaign of 1000 li, the combined cost to the people and the public exchequer will be 1000 jin per day. There will be widespread disruption at home and abroad, people will fall exhausted at the roadside and as many as 700,000 families will be unable to do their daily work.

Spending years in stalemated campaigning, which could be settled in one day's decisive battle, because you are too miserly to lay out 1000 silver pieces in rewards to discover the enemy's circumstances: this is inhumane in the extreme. It is not the behaviour of a leader of the people, nor of a true prop to the ruler or a master of victory. For what enables a wise ruler and an able general to attack decisively and to succeed where ordinary men fail, is foreknowledge. And foreknowledge cannot be found by consulting the spirits, or by comparing similar situations. It is not to be found by measuring the movements of heaven and the earth; it is to be obtained from men who have accurate knowledge of the enemy's situation.

---

[34] Sunzi's understanding of the necessity of an effective intelligence network, its efficient organization and the various levels of expendability of its agents is chillingly calculating...and modern.

故用間有五:有因間, 有內間, 有反間, 有死間, 有生間。五間俱起, 莫知其道, 是謂神紀, 人君之寶也。

因間者, 因其鄉人而用之。內間者, 因其官人而用之。反間者, 因其敵間而用之。死間者, 為誑事于外, 令吾聞知之, 而傳于敵間也。生間者, 反報也。

故三軍之事, 莫親于間, 賞莫厚于間, 事莫密于間。非聖智不能用間, 非仁義不能使間, 非微妙不能得間之實。微哉!微哉!無所不用間也。

To this end there are five types of spy you may use: the local spy, the internal spy, the converted spy, the expendable spy and the permanent spy. If you use all five types, no-one can fathom their machinations – it is a kind of divine organization, and is a ruler's greatest treasure.

Local spies are recruited from the enemy's peasantry, and internal spies from their court officials. Converted spies mean using the enemy's own spies against them. Expendable spies are those who are fed false information so that it may be picked up by the enemy's own spies. Permanent spies are the ones who concentrate on bringing back reports.

Thus in your whole army, none should be closer to you than your spies; none should be more richly rewarded; and no secret more closely guarded than your spy network. Spies must be used sagaciously and treated with benevolence and virtue; and you must use the utmost subtlety to be sure of obtaining true reports from your spies. Subtlety is the key! There are no circumstances where spies cannot be used.

" Spies must be used sagaciously and treated with benevolence... "

間事未發，而先聞者，間與所告者兼死。

凡軍之所欲擊，城之所欲攻，人之所欲殺，必先知其守將、左右、謁者、門者、舍人之姓名，令吾間必索知之。

必索敵人之間來間我者，因而利之，導而舍之，故反間可得而用也。因是而知之，故鄉間、內間可得而使也；因是而知之，故死間為誑事可使告敵；因是而知之，故生間可使如期。五間之事，君必知之，知之必在于反間，故反間不可不厚也。昔殷之興也，伊摯在夏；周之興也，呂牙在殷。

故惟明君賢將能以上智為間者，必成大功。此兵之要，三軍之所恃而動也。

" *When you find the enemy's agents spying on you, offer them bribes...* "

If a spy lets slip information before a plan has come to fruition, then both the spy and anyone he has told must be put to death. Whether you wish to destroy an army, attack a city or assassinate somebody, the first essential is to identify by name the general in command, his attendants, his aides, his gatekeepers and bodyguards. You should order your spies to obtain this information.

When you the find the enemy's agents spying on you, offer them bribes, lavish care on them and lodge them handsomely. Thus they may become converted spies and be of use to you. It is through these converted spies that you will be able to recruit local spies and internal spies. It is through them that your expendable spies will feed false reports to the enemy. And it is also through them that your permanent spies will be able to act as occasion demands. A ruler must know how to employ all five kinds of spy, and this understanding comes necessarily from the converted spy. Therefore treat none more generously than your converted spies. In ancient times, the rise of the Yin was due to the work of Yi Zhi, formerly in the employ of the Xia; and the rise of the Zhou was due to the work of Lu Ya,[35] formerly in the employ of the Yin.

A wise ruler or an able general must select only the most intelligent men to act as his spies and then he will be sure of achieving great things. This is a necessity of war, and an army depends on it to act.

---

[35] The Yin is an alternative name for the Shang Dynasty (c1500–1050 BCE), the second Bronze Age Dynasty which overthrew the original Xia (c2000–c1500 BCE). Yi Zhi, also known as Yi Yin, was a Xia statesman instrumental in its downfall who took high office under the Shang. Similarly, Lu Ya who helped overthrow the Shang and then served under the succeeding Zhou Dynasty (1050–770 BCE).

Index